CW00972575

reflections
for Dawn, Day & Dusk

reflections
for Dawn, Day & Dusk

by Anthony Strano

ETERNITY INK

reflections *by* Anthony Strano

Published by Eternity Ink   Email: bkmedia@ozemail.com.au

©2001 Brahma Kumaris Raja Yoga Centres Australia Inc.

First edition November 2001

Reprinted September 2004

ISBN 0 9587230 4 4

This book has been produced by the Brahma Kumaris World Spiritual University, a non-profit organisation, with the aim of sharing spiritual knowledge as a community service for the personal growth of individuals. The Brahma Kumaris World Spiritual University exists to serve the family of humanity: to assist individuals to discover and experience their own spirituality and personal growth; to understand the significance and consequences of individual actions and global interactions; and to reconnect and strengthen the eternal relationship with the Supreme Soul, the spiritual parent.

contents

8

welcome to the journey of spirituality

The reflections in this booklet are offered as signs or guides for the dedicated spiritual pilgrims who are familiar with the head winds of life. These pilgrims learn to face all situations as opportunities to learn about themselves, remove inner burdens and move closer to God and perfection. The emerging relationships with God, in all their forms and magnificence, protect their path. Victory is guaranteed.

At the start of the journey, new pilgrims, empowered by spiritual study, take on the mountains of opportunity with an enthusiasm that is at times ignorant of the efforts required to achieve the heights of success. In contrast, experienced pilgrims may tire and slacken their efforts for inner perfection, as each step forward introduces a higher gradient. As the spiritual study continues, it becomes important to prevent these habits and routines, even spiritual ones, enticing pilgrims to accept lower aims or attitudes. It is important not to lower the aim or the vision of what is attainable when old habits or routines evoke complacency or doubt.

Bearing in mind that along the path the focus of effort will change, five guiding principles are useful to keep in mind. They underpin the change process. They are:

1. Check on and dissolve again any ego or "I-ness". Such an attitude taints the purity of an action and creates discontent.

2. Be content with everything, everyone, every scene of life no matter how imperfect it appears. Everything is as it should be and, if inner change is necessary, work with patient love and gentle determination.

3. Keep digging deep within the self. Keep digging till the silent spring is found. This spring of original goodness, once opened, will keep bubbling inside, refreshing the pilgrim with clarity and simplicity.

4. Not think about or be with God for selfish motives. Selfishness is the shadow that blurs this relationship.

5. Practise inner stability of the mind and refuse to let old emotions create reactions and eruptions that blind the soul to the next step and later bring regret when everything has calmed down. If mistakes occur, use the mistake to intensify the will to not repeat foolishness. If the soul has courage, God and life definitely co-operate and time blesses us.

Anthony Strano

January 2001

To use this book

Step Back

Become the observer for a few minutes. Watch the mind; observe thoughts; check their speed, their criticism, anger, stress. Slow them down. As you step back from your mind and your situation, things fall into perspective and you begin to feel calm.

Step In

As you enter the calm state, you open the treasure of balance and harmony. With this one thought – I am a being of peace – the mind will unplug itself from external negative sockets and plug into the self. Now select a daily reflection from this book. Each reflection is written in the first person so that you can apply it to yourself.

Step Up

Now let your mind rise to God. In nature, plants rise as the rays of the sun touch them. Also your divine potential can only be realised when touched by God's light. You feel the peace and love flow in and then from that spiritual height, your love and peace flows out.

Step Out

Feel how your vision is different, infused with generosity and beyond pettiness.

You reach out to all. You continue with the day's activities.

Dawn – greeting myself and God

Be still. Let silence flow

then all that I need will come to me, like the dawn.

To be in tune with myself, I go beyond

the sound of thoughts,

the sound of feelings

and especially beyond

the sounds of what, how, when, who and why.

Make time for time.

Unclutter the day and create windows of silence for the mind.

Windows, which catch the light of peace and clarity.

Windows which reflect the stillness and calmness of eternity.

Windows which let oxygen into the mind.

I cannot know all.

I cannot do all.

I cannot own all.

I cannot be all – just a part of the whole.

When I discover that part,

contentment floods the soul

and serenity reigns in the mind.

To create permanent peace, I need to know myself.

This self-respect will dissolve the dependence

that creates mixed emotions;

sometimes close,

sometimes distant,

sometimes loving,

sometimes rejecting.

Conflict is the combined result

of dependence, expectation and selfish desires.

To create true harmony, I let go of expecting

to be understood, to be considered, to be recognised,

Instead, I accept that things cannot always happen as I wish.

I am learning to ask questions and let go of wanting answers.

Relevant questions are like brooms

that sweep the mind and create a clean space.

The mind needs clean space.

Answers enter clean space.

When I am too focused on answers, I lose them.

In the early morning, when all is still and silent,

thoughts begin to stir.

A thought is a drop of energy

and when it is focused and directed towards God

each drop, grows and swells

and soon the mind becomes an ocean

flooded with perfect peace and quiet joy.

A gift from the Supreme.

The more I am an observer,

the more I can be honest and quiet.

When there is honesty and quietness,

the strength of God comes into me.

Every morning,

I let my heart concentrate on the qualities of God.

These qualities become the blueprint for my day.

Every day I need this exercise to stay free

of mirages and colours that weaken me.

In the silence of the morning,

I remind myself to not believe a wasteful thought.

If I believe it, it becomes reality.

Truth comes into me

the more I keep myself free from my own thinking.

Observing myself is possible when there is detachment.

In yoga, this consciousness is expressed by

I see but don't see, I hear but don't hear.

There is awareness

but nothing penetrates the mind to make it negative.

Let God in so I see myself as I am.

I do not have to prove myself.

I can't anyway.

I am human,

I am vulnerable to fear, ego, jealousy and anger.

He accepts this

and as long as I accept these things about myself,

He will guide me out of this labyrinth – if I want a way out.

If not... He will wait.

He will not think me a failure.

God is my Friend.

He does not see failure.

He sees the future.

Allow God to do.

Give God permission to act.

Allow life to be.

Why do I think that it all depends on me...

On me getting it right...

On me calculating the accuracy of every step...

On me...

Let it be!

Sow the seed of whatever inspires.

Whatever is my responsibility,

whatever can be my contribution then let it be...

Let it be.

Let life assist.

God is there to co-operate and not to test me or analyse me.

God's co-operation helps me be me.

This morning there is great joy in being alone

and taking the silent journey into light.

My Spiritual Father is Light. His world is Light.

His Thoughts are Light.

In the pure silence of the morning, He turns me into light.

He inspires me to become pure, to be honest and to be true.

Now I observe myself with love.

Now I teach myself with love.

Let me change and keep changing.

Then all things will change.

What does God wish of me today?

I shall open myself

to such an extent where God can give me an honest answer.

Otherwise He will keep quiet and wait until I am ready.

This supreme and patient quietness is misunderstood often,

so God is asked

"Why don't you listen, why don't you do something?"

My Eternal Friend,

what blind spot can I let go of today

in order to come closer to you, to be like you,

to serve with nothing else except your Light?

God, who are you? Who are you God?

I am the Great Musician

and you are the instrument in this orchestra of life.

Let me play my song through you;

the Song of Truth,

the Song of Freedom,

the Song of Peace.

This Song has unique rhythm as it plays through you.

When each soul, each instrument, plays a unique note

the melody is pure sound vibrating across the earth.

All creation joins in this eternal rhythm and dances.

To dance like this, remember who you are.

Remember who you are, then you will know who I am.

A blessing is an inspiration from God.

A blessing is a window in my mind

through which I see the eternity of truth,

through which I glimpse at the blueprint of my potential,

through which I realise that I am born to reach the ultimate.

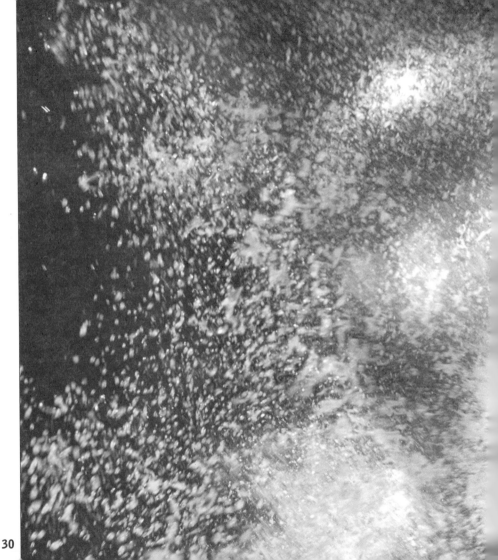

Day – connecting with others

Whatever is happening or not happening

I remain calm and confident

because it is all appropriate and somehow, it is all necessary.

Whatever is said, whatever is done,

have the strength not to be influenced.

Remain beyond opinion, praise and defamation

and have the strength to remain caring.

I detach and understand dependence.

Otherwise, I only move forward if I have approval.

Then I am never free to think and act as I choose.

I do not get upset with anyone,

because the difficulty begins with me and can only finish with me.

Others simply mirror

what I have refused to acknowledge in myself.

But I cannot avoid myself forever.

Sooner or later the mirror of time reflects reality,

begging to be seen.

I step back from reactions of blame and accusation,

and avoid the temptation of hopelessness,

of wanting to isolate and to justify my 'rightness'.

I no longer take support from those

whom I know will agree with my indignation and dissatisfaction.

I am willing, with all courage and humility,

to accept and to believe it is truly time that "I change".

Remain easy.

Easiness is strength.

Easiness means open, accepting, flexible, confident,

and trusting the process.

I do not have to prove myself or convince anyone.

True goodness achieves without assistance or insistence.

I need courage and respect to communicate.

To speak courageously and respectfully means

to say what I mean and what I feel

without inhibiting another soul.

Sometimes I speak my opinion with courage

but forget the feelings of the other party.

In this way, I oppress truth.

Sometimes my respect is timid

so then I neither express my opinion

nor do I say what I really mean.

Then I feel suppressed.

Courage is born from faith in the self

and respect from faith in others.

The religion of life is transformation.

Nature is constantly transforming herself in repeating cycles.

Seasons of change which create, sustain, destroy

and then again create, sustain, destroy.

Nothing becomes extinct but all things are transformed.

Even my breath is a link to eternity,

not to death, as some think.

Let one not trespass

or stray into minds and ideas that are foreign,

adapting to them simply because of opinion and fear.

That would be like a bird trying to live life as a fish.

When there are bad feelings or mistrust

then a genuine mistake is perceived as a plot,

a calculated violence, and part of a bigger scheme.

Do not pressure, cajole, demand

threaten or oblige someone

into a position or action they are not ready for

nor into something they have not chosen.

Any type of force quickly creates a wall of resentment

that later will take a lot of time to demolish.

Trust can be lost in a moment, but can take years to rebuild.

When people are allowed to choose,

all the best comes from them spontaneously.

To use events of the past to prove how right I was after all,

to remind someone of their past,

means to increase their load of guilt and regret.

It makes it impossible for them

to forgive themselves and start again.

The reason I remind them is to punish the one

who did not listen, who did not accept or value me.

I have not forgotten

and I make sure that person does not forget.

Is this the way I want to be?

To become tight, hard, forceful,

insisting on a way, or on an idea defeats the purpose.

Being this way, I only think

– to survive, to defend, to protect – myself.

This rigidity creates aggression

and paralyses all movement forward.

This self-attachment, blended with pettiness,

breeds constant loss.

Is this my style?

Arrogant self-confidence, in the striving for success,

crushes everything and everyone on their path.

Based in fear, this arrogance cannot be kind or step back.

A step back or allowing space

is interpreted as a loss, a weakness or even an insult

that is why it feels obliged to keep crushing,

pushing and rushing

towards the goal at all and any cost.

True self-confidence cannot have ego.

Egoless self-confidence comes with humility and pure intention.

This self-confidence is compassionate,

flexible, easy, light and gives space to others.

People think that what they say or direct is 'right'.
When they use their position to force their ideas,
their blindness curbs the confidence and freedom of others
by cleverly imposing, either forcefully or diplomatically,
a biased view of truth.
Narrow viewpoints never inspire co-operation.

It is wrong to try to prove myself right against anyone.
The most sincere thing is to be right in the self.
To feel pleasure or a sense of victory
about the self being right and the other wrong,
develops an unhealthy self-righteousness.
This is the greatest deception.

Dissolve ego and forcefulness and let things be.

Dissolve anger and reaction.

Observe and cultivate trust.

Dissolve the distraction of looking outward.

Go inside and touch base.

Be free.

Desire and reaction are like twins.

As soon as one is born, the other arrives quickly.

The desire for recognition makes my effort dishonest

and the quality of the task is polluted.

Inevitably the integrity of the self is lost.

Desires, like the many-headed dragon, nourish unhappiness.

They aim to fill me but, keep me empty

to the extent that each desire is fulfilled.

This is a paradox not understood easily

until I see that desire works through habit.

Habit is the huge old dragon that does not permit realisation;

does not admit personal weakness; does not perceive self.

"I want"; "I need" and "You have to give me"

are hungry dragons with a fathomless stomach.

Whatever I feed them increases their appetite.

Contentment comes when I dissolve these desires

that always want something from someone.

This contentment allows me to live

aware of the meaning in each scene,

in every human encounter,

in each breath of time.

"You don't co-operate"; "You don't listen";

"You don't understand"; "I am not valued enough"

are all accusations and demands of the egocentric mind

which eventually finds itself unheard, unwanted, alone.

That is, until that moment when the mind hears itself

and wants to be with God.

When I feel victimised and preoccupied

with what others say or might be saying...

When I produce evidence to prove how badly others treat me...

When I complain of being controlled...

I am dependent.

No more does difficulty or negativity tempt me

to leave a situation or person.

I learn to grow through it.

When I sow the seed of determined thought,

I grow

by accepting the necessity of changing my mental position.

The change in position changes my growth pattern.

I grow into my original truth and my authenticity.

Then my example flows into the hearts and minds of others.

They glow with hope and inspiration, thinking "We can also

become that".

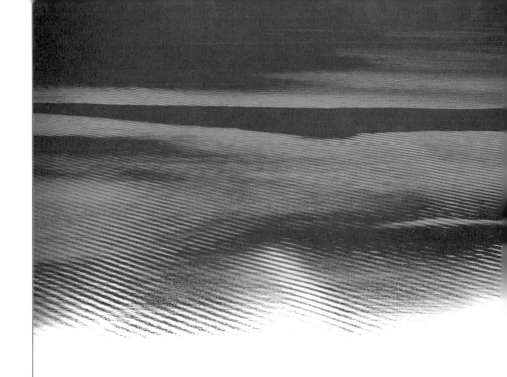

When there is conflict what position should I take?

If I yield too much, there are feelings of suppression.

If I assert too much, there is danger of domination.

The best position is to step out of both and go up above.

Look at everything from there.

Observe, rather than entangle the self in struggle.

As I observe, I detach.

I become lighter and clearer.

Nothing appears to be a problem.

From up above I understand

that no-one is 'bad' or for that matter, 'good'.

This wisdom creates patience and understanding;

compassion rather than reaction.

From above, I find balance.

I do not take sides.

Having conquered bias, I remain fair and just.

When I act, I will know how to

yield without suppression and assert without dominance.

I am disoriented.

No anchor. No base.

Nothing to hold on to except trust and stillness.

Patience is born.

My primary thought is to control and direct outcome

but instead I trust my destiny

and a voice says "... transformation is fun."

Who lacks time?

I may lack time to do things

but there is always time to be a better person.

There is always time to be more patient,

more generous, more tolerant and more forgiving,

because no day can pass without need to practise these values.

Time is always giving me these opportunities.

Can I say that I do not have time for them?

When the focus falls on a soul's weaknesses,

the potential to realise virtue and value

in myself, in others and in tasks, is ruined.

To make an environment positive, I focus on 'good'.

Happiness is not possible when I am alone. Only when I am a member of the community can expression of my individuality be genuine and non-intrusive and benefit the collective. Then my happiness is lasting.

If I am asking others to show me love and respect;

become worthy to receive love and respect.

If I am waiting for others to be virtuous and understanding;

become what I want others to be.

If I am expecting others to give me their best;

accept whatever they can give and begin from there.

If I am holding onto others

convinced that they are the source of my happiness;

let go of these addictive supports. Be free.

Learn

to become

to change

to accept

to let go

Then I experience love.

Dusk – honouring life and God

All things have their time. All things have their answers.

All things have their right to be.

Accepting this reality, all things come into harmony.

Wherever I am, I am a guest.

Whatever I do, I am an instrument.

Whatever I have, I am a trustee.

Time is my instrument of expression.

Without the flow of time I remain locked,

like the seed that is not planted in the earth.

I, the flower, wait for the opportunity of time.

Contentment comes and only comes

when I finally decide to live as I am meant to live.

To be what I know I am;

to love others as they are;

to be attentive to the needs of now.

Contentment means

I am no longer clogged with thoughts of others.

Beyond fear, desire and pretension, I enjoy joy.

To forget my uniqueness

creates a lack of purpose and meaning.

To be attached to my uniqueness

creates arrogance that cancels benevolence.

The universe recognises my unique contribution to life.

I shall too.

Self-esteem comes only when I am not attached to myself.

When attachment to myself enters,

it pollutes the purity of any action, thought or word.

Self-esteem lies in non-attachment to actions.

I do nothing. Everything is being done.

The more I am aware of the truth, the more silent I remain

because genuine truth proves itself in the course of time.

Corrections, proofs, insistence

are never points of revealing truth.

Often they are masks,

camouflaging personal irritation and bias.

There is only one thing that matters – that nothing really matters
except to keep serenity of mind and speech.
Only serenity safeguards dignity.

I do not need to see what is wrong.

By choice I go inside the self

and with compassion put things right,

silently and humbly, if possible and when possible.

Otherwise to jump into a moralistic reaction

multiplies the wrong a thousand fold.

'Quality' time means I have natural attention on myself so that any improvement benefits me and others. 'Quality' relationship means there is no selfish motive or need. 'Quality' relationship brings me to spiritual empowerment. Spiritual power is the capacity to realise the self and keep myself free of selfish influence. Realisation penetrates my being. When there is 'quality' realisation, the sense of commitment is strong and there is attention to sincere application. When I have 'clever' realisations, it brings superficial change which can be sidetracked by excuses and circumstances.

Let each one learn their own lesson

in their own way, at their own time.

Stop being the judge and become a friend.

A friend lightens the load.

A friend encourages newness.

A friend helps to forget.

Often anger is an unfilled expectation.

It is an attempt to try to find from others

what I cannot find in myself.

Never let go of the effort.

Never let go of the aim.

Never let go of the faith to change.

Hold on.

Keep holding on no matter what,

because as love and time guide and protect,

the goal is attained.

Ultimately, I only have what I truly am.

That is strength.

If I have borrowed strength from a name,

a role, a position, a group or a person,

there comes a point when it all dissolves and I will feel empty,

floundering for a sense of identity and

desperate for self-esteem.

I go 'inside' and find myself.

All support, all wisdom, all solutions are already there.

Simply, I need to remember.

I anchor my being in silence and focus my mind on the Divine.

I absorb the blessing of the truth.

Then there is the courage to make all necessary changes

without flinching, without excuse, without show.

I do not wish to beg, to plead, to need or demand from God.

I wish to be free from these words and attitudes.

Need creates dependency.

Then there cannot be respect or maturity in a relationship,

whether it is with God or humans.

In dependency there is blame.

I blame God for not making it happen the way I want;

not co-operating in the things I expect;

not producing the miracles I need.

I blame people in the same way.

Is this sacrilege?

The strong give.
The weak expect.

The strong change.
The weak complain.

The strong forgive.
The weak resent.

The strong create.
The weak hesitate.

The stronger flow.
The weaker measure.

The stronger yield.
The weaker tighten.

The stronger allow.
The weaker limit.

The stronger bend.
The weaker break.

The weakest clamour and announce.
The strongest calm and quieten.

When the mind is still, silent, detached

then thought becomes a thread that stitches itself to God.

To be combined with God brings a consciousness

beyond matter, time, even thoughts.

This is enlightenment.

Honest communication with God means

to meet as I am, how I am.

God is like the laundry man – he soaks the soul in the warm water of knowledge, adding the detergent of virtues; then washes, rinses, rubs, wrings, dries and irons it. The mind especially needs ironing. With ironing the wrinkles of the past, of waste, of doubt, of fear, of looking at others are removed completely. The mind is clean – ready for spiritual service.

Do not get tired in the effort

to be better, to be realised, to be true.

Tiredness comes because there is too much self –

I and my.

I do, I know, I have.

My weakness, my effort and my achievement.

I remain still, watch and feel the miracle of change in me

that God can accomplish with my consent.

'Mine' is the source of all conflict. It blocks my compassion.

God speaking...

You strive to be true. Your freedom is guaranteed.

You have decided to know yourself so I am bound to help you.

You planted the seed of pure courage so you are being filled.

You are growing with light yet becoming smaller

– a tiny point of bliss.

You hold the ocean in a thought.

Each thought of yours flows

with freshness, vitality and enthusiasm,

cooling minds, awakening hearts, stirring faith in themselves.

The flow of mercy glows in your eyes,

through your hands, through your light.

This glow leads others to safety.

Purpose is lit.

The world pleads for this light

that heals each human heart, each human mind.

Are you ready?

Raja yoga meditation

Habits, the deep addictions of the soul, like emperors who own a kingdom, rule us. Habits, over time, gain supremacy over logic and reason, doing as they like without thinking or caring for the true well-being of the person. The mind is the throne of these emperors and, like tyrants, they usurp peace and clarity. They domineer without sweetness or sympathy.

The aim in Raja Yoga meditation is to change our habits and to dethrone these tyrants. To do this, we need an intellect filled with spiritual knowledge. We need to use this third eye of understanding. Through knowledge, reason returns to the human soul and gives it the power to conquer the tyrants of the mind. Knowledge is necessary, but silence is also necessary. In silence we can make connection with God, which gives us the strength to regain our lost dignity. Our original dignity lies in being the ruler of ourselves. Raja Yoga is about learning to master ourselves, regaining our inner kingdom and regaining our throne.

About the author

Anthony Strano is the Director of the Brahma Kumaris in
Turkey and Greece. Born in Australia in 1951, he graduated
from Macquarie University in Sydney with a Bachelor of Arts
and a Diploma of Education.

A spiritual seeker all his life, Anthony became a student of the
Brahma Kumaris in 1977. Now, he is one of the Spiritual
University's most experienced teachers.

Over the years, he has travelled widely, sharing the knowledge
he has gathered. He has run seminars and workshops
throughout Europe and Australia on positive thinking and
stress-free living, on education and values, on science and
spirituality.

An arts festival, organised by Anthony and dedicated to the
United Nations International Year of Poverty in 1996,
demonstrated how the exploration of the ways in which theatre,
literature, music and fine arts can be tools for overcoming
poverty of the spirit.

His own spiritual journey is at the heart of his existence.
Anthony considers himself always to be a student as well as a
teacher.

ETERNITY INK

Other Eternity Ink meditation books, tapes and CDs available. For a catalogue contact:
Eternity Ink, 77 Allen Street, Leichhardt NSW Australia 2040
Email: bkmedia@ozemail.com.au
www.bkmedia.com.au
www.brahmakumaris.com.au or www.bkwsu.com

Eternity Ink is publisher for the Brahma Kumaris World Spiritual University.
If you wish to find out about the free meditation courses offered by the
Brahma Kumaris World Spiritual University, contact the main centre closest to you:

UK:	International Co-ordinating Office,	
	65 Pound Lane, London, NW10 2HH, UK	
	Tel (20) 8727 3350	Email: london@bkwsu.com
AUSTRALIA:	78 Alt Street, Ashfield, Sydney NSW 2131	
	Tel (2) 9716 7066	Email: indra@brahmakumaris.com.au
BRAZIL:	R. Dona Germaine Burchard, 589 – Sao Paulo, SP 05002-062,	
	Tel (11) 3864 3694	Email: saopaulo@bkumaris.org.br
CHINA:	17 Dragon Road, Causeway Bay, Hong Kong	
	Tel (852) 2806 3008	Email: rajainfo@rajayoga.com.hk
INDIA:	25 New Rohtak Road, Karol Bagh, New Delhi, 1100055	
	Tel (11) 2355 0355	Email: bkpbd@vsnl.com
KENYA:	PO Box 12349, Maua Close, off Parklands Road, Westlands, Nairobi	
	Tel (2) 3743 572	Email: bkwsugm@holidaybazaar.com
RUSSIA:	2 Gospitalnaya Ploscha, Building 1, Moscow 111020	
	Tel (95) 263 02 47	Email: bkwsu@mail.ru
USA:	Global Harmony House, 46 South Middle Neck Road, Great Neck NY 11021	
	Tel (516) 773 0971	Email: newyork@bkwsu.com